Social media marketing Brand ROI

By Ananthanarayanan V

Personal message from the Author:

Dear Friends,

Thank you very much for purchasing a copy of my book, "Social media marketing brand ROI".

I, am Ananthanarayanan V (Ananth) born and raised in Mumbai, India.

I love working with brands and technology products.

I enjoy running as a hobby and am an avid writer and blogger. I have published two books earlier, one in 2007 called Expressions which was a coffee table poetry book and was covered by the Times of India team in Mumbai and the second book in 2010 called "Kings are made, not just born" published on Amazon Kindle.

Academic credentials:

- PGCPM – IIM Indore (Outstanding credentials in Marketing research)
- PGDJMC – IGNOU
- Diploma Advertising & PR – Welingkars institute of Management studies

- Diploma in Advanced Animation and VFX – IIDT
- Technical certifications – Brainbench, USA
- B.Com – Mumbai University

Over the past eight to 10 years, I have had the privilege of working with some of the best brands in the industry today. That coupled with a passion in the field of digital marketing, I embarked on this journey to start my own digital marketing and social media creative services agency called Techdivine Creative Services.

In the year 2010 we registered our company and its office in Mumbai, India. In the past four years, we have catered to over 30 brands across 16 industries in 3 countries.

As a company we have delivered social media and digital marketing campaigns across industries and countries with power packed measurable results delivered by our agency, few of which are mentioned below –

- 31 % conversion on actual sales online
- 65 % brand mentions increase
- 23 % increase in footfalls
- Real-time social conversations to sales conversions
- SEO Google page ranking No 1 across three different countries search engine in less than a week using appropriate and approved strategies
- High brand engagement
- 4,000 Plus database generation of blog subscribers in a span of six months focused from a geo based campaign
- Brand monitoring for brand mentions and complete campaign control
- Emailer to lead conversion and to sales conversion campaigns

Over the years, I have been invited across elite corporate brands and institutes for sharing my expertise and experience in the field of technology, creative design and digital marketing. In case you would like me to conduct a digital marketing seminar or social media workshop for your organization, please feel free to reach me.

I hope you find this book resourceful, insightful and refreshing to read.

I have shared some of our campaign insights, case studies, marketing tool process across industries empowered by digital and social media marketing campaigns.

There is also a surprise waiting for you as you near the end of the book.

Do share your comments, feedback and views with me. Looking forward to hearing from you.

Feel free to connect with me across social profile sites on –

- Facebook – https://www.facebook.com/AnanthV9
- Twitter - https://www.twitter.com/AnanthV9
- LinkedIn – http://in.linkedin.com/in/techdivine
- Personal Blog – www.ananthv9.wordpress.com

Have a wonderful year ahead.

Be Well

Ananth V

Founder & CEO
Techdivine Creative Services

To my parents, for their patience

and their faith in me.

Social media marketing Brand ROI

"The aim of marketing is to know and understand the customer so well the product or service fits him and sells itself. ~ Peter Drucker"

Welcome to 'Social media marketing Brand ROI'

This book will be useful for CMO's, CEO's, CTO's and senior marketing management professionals who are key decision makers planning or strategizing digital marketing campaigns with specific goals in mind.

It deals with core aspects of integrating campaigns with the focus to deliver Return On Investment (ROI) while co-creating value for end users with personalization.

CONTENTS:

- What is social media marketing?
- What is social media quotient (SMQ)? How do I measure my brand's SMQ?
- Will social media marketing campaign really help my company or brand?
- How to get started?
- Which social networking site to choose?
- What type of messages really appeals to end users on social media? (How do contests, freebies, etc impact them?) – "RESEARCH" based insights
- How safe is it to have an engaging relationship in real-time with my end users?
- Trends: Should I be a part of the frenzy, just because everyone is talking about it?
- What do I track and how often do I measure my social media digital campaigns across my brand's varied marketing strategies?

- What do I do with my company's traditional marketing strategies meanwhile?
- Best time to post on social media
- Sales conversions and social media ROI metrics
  - LTV (lifetime value of a customer)
  - CPC (Cost per customer)
  - CAC (Customer acquisition cost)
  - Your SMQ® – Your Social media quotient tools and process

- "Why would users online engage with YOUR BRAND on SOCIAL MEDIA?" - Research across 1,000 from 9 industries:
  - 1,000 users surveyed across 9 Industries (Hotels and hospitality, Movies, Real-estate, Retail, Finance & banking solutions, Publishing, IT institutes, Management institutes and Trading & Broking) for their valuable insights based on industry specific brand pages across social networking sites on:
    - Time spent on social networking sites and time spent interacting with brand pages
    - Which social networking sites do you use the most?
    - Referrals, re-sell, upgrade & brand loyalty: How and what makes them BUY?
    - Why would you engage with a brand?
- Test your SOCIAL MEDIA BRAND quotient. The questions are based on this book
- **WIN** a surprise gift from me!

BONUS Content:

- Social media misconceptions cleared
- Creative story telling using social media

- Power SEO – Simple tips for quick website optimization
- Key branding rules online
- Don't make a social faux pas

& also few useful resources, posts and 'case study' links for downloads

<u>ROI that we will be looking into:</u>

- SEO (Search engine optimization)
- Higher Brand reach
- Quality brand engagement
- Reaching target specific consumers
- Brand monitoring
- What to measure and how to measure it?
- Lead enquiries and 'Sales' conversions

<u>Let us begin:</u>

Social media marketing: Is it really for BRAND You?

Prior to starting any social media or digital marketing campaign, it is extremely imperative as a member of the company's management, board and as one of the key decision makers to ask this question to your team members -

'Is Social Media Marketing really for our brand? If yes, what is our brand's social media quotient?'

<u>To understand this, you would first need to know:</u>

What is social media marketing?

If your answer is 'Social media marketing is the process of gaining website traffic or making users share your content and be more popular using or through social media sites with fans, followers or likes' then it's time to un-learn and start afresh with this book right here and right now.

I have a very simple yet unambiguous definition for 'social media marketing' as follows:

> Social media marketing is a well researched scientific marketing process with a clear goal to cater to specific management and organizational needs and at the same time deliver high value in terms of personalization of services to end users in real-time while engaging with your brand.

Now that we have a much simpler understanding of what social media marketing is, let us look into what is social media quotient?

Social media quotient is your company's measurable metric when online.

It includes your power to engage with audiences and at the same time generate high brand loyalty and empowers your brand to convert prospects into consumers in real-time.

What social media quotient is NOT?

It is not the number of 'likes' or 'follows' of your brand across any social networking site unless and until you see more than 50% of your fans and or followers engaging with your brand on a daily basis. For eg. If your brand has 10,000 followers on facebook and 300 or less of them engage with you on a daily basis, it is a poor quality metric in terms of social media. Rather, have a smaller number of real and organic followers who interact with your brand with genuine interest consistently. This also helps to dodge the fear of spam followers or fake followers who either contribute nothing to your brand or have a negative impact on your social page.

Let us now look into the question that you as a brand and a key decision maker need to ask:

'Are you just a part of the Social media frenzy or is this market potential really going to help you?'

Before you jump into a social media marketing campaign because everyone else seems to be doing it, ask yourself few questions like:

- Where did I hear about it?

  If it is from your competitors site or your technical team make sure you pay attention to it and understand its needs and demands before making any decision? Why is this important for my company?

- Can application of this channel or medium really help me improve my business?

  For this you need to know what this process can really do for you. Then share the insights of this with your board including your marketing and delivery team. Why? Because if your promise cannot be delivered, better not make yourself more visible, at least not right now or not without hiring professionals specialized in this field who will be able to help you plan the same.

- Is this medium safe to keep my brand protected?

  This is very vital to know, for which an organization usually ends up handling the key responsibilities of running these powerful marketing campaigns to professional agencies. For eg. As a company policy the first process we implement prior to starting any social media or digital campaign for our client brand partners is 'brand monitoring'.

- Is my organization willing to give the time needed to build the brand across multiple platforms?

  If the answer is a no, then your answer is to prolong with the traditional media process that seems to work fine for your company as of now. It's very simple, if you do not trust it enough to invest your time in it, then it is best advised not to get into it right now. The first rule of social media marketing is – Brands have a much more important role than ever before, i.e. to connect with the customer within.

- If your organization is willing to engage in the technology tools of today, how can your team leverage your existing intellectual properties to further add value to your brand, product and service?

- Finally, the most important aspect of all - what do you plan to achieve with the social media marketing campaign?

"The purpose of a business is to create a customer. ~ Peter Drucker"

Every campaign of social media and digital marketing is measurable, so make sure to have clearly defined goals like for eg.

- Increase leads by 15% in the first quarter
- Optimize five keywords for top ranking SEO results online and offsite in three months

- Build a brand following on facebook with 60% Social media quotient[*note 1] for my brand.
- Increase leads to sales conversions by 10% in the first quarter
- Increase footfalls by 65% in the first quarter
- Encourage and initiate at least 1,000 check-ins at the event in the first one hour

Once you are able to answer these questions you can either set up a good team of skilled resources with a combination of strong marketing skills, analytical bent of mind who are technologically sound to run the campaigns for you or you can hire professional agencies to plan it as per your organizational goals.

A brief intro on "How to get started"

- Profile your product, audience, market and your goals

- Decide on the mediums and channel to implement your social media marketing campaigns

- Clearly define to measure your social media quotient across brands and services

- Set timelines that are realistic

- Plan, design, implement, measure, track and reinforce with improvisations if needed.

- Get feedback, work on the feedback and constantly improvise

"In business, the idea of measuring what you are doing, picking the measurements that count like customer satisfaction and performance... you thrive on that. ~ Bill Gates"

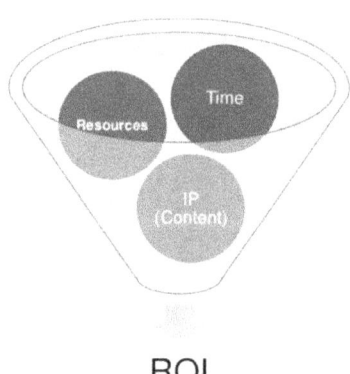

ROI

Which social networking site to choose?

Branding has since ages been an integral part of every corporate strategy and over the decades, organizations have invested heavily to make the best of the available branding tools for communicating news and information about their products and services with consumers and prospects.

Recently, with the advent of social media marketing as a powerful tool, brands have embraced social networking sites like Facebook, Twitter, Google Plus, Pinterest, Instagram etc as not merely a medium to communicate, but as a core strategy and process to engage consumers and increase brand reach.

So how do you decide which social networking sites to focus on?

The most important aspect as an organization that you being a key decision maker need to remember while planning a social media or digital marketing campaign is –

Social media is not about websites. It was, is and will always be about people. People buy from people they trust, so 'Humanize your BRAND'.

This will give you a tremendous edge to have real-time brand conversations with higher loyalty with prospects and consumers. This gives us an all new perspective of the term "BRANDING".

It is never merely BRANDING which appeals to users, but the process within that helps them actually converse with the brand on a personal level. Also, when you as an organization are able to humanize your brand, you would realize that your end users not only buy from you but end up becoming your brand ambassadors online.

"What type of messages really appeals to end users on social media?"

We did a small research with a group of 100 of our corporate blog readers with following Demographics: We got feedback from 63 readers on the same: DETAILS of the research:

Cities: Mumbai, Delhi, Kanpur, Chennai, Bangalore, USA (Chicago, New York), UAE (Sharjah & Dubai), Singapore & UK: London, Birmingham

Age groups: 15 – 50

Male to Female: 1.17:1

Education: High school students, College Graduates, Undergrads, working Professionals & professionals with Doctorate

Industries we analyzed using these consumer insights:

- Fashion & Retail
- IT
- Automobile
- Hospitality Restaurants
- MLM Business
- Industrial products
- Banking
- Investment and Finance
- NGO
- Event management
- Infrastructure
- Personal Branding and or Celebrity Branding
- Publishing (Print and Digital)
- Sports

From our research, we were further able to understand the "WHY" behind "WHY some messages have a powerful impact to readers or prospects" and to what type of "Communication, Images and Incentives" do users have a higher probability to respond to a call of action etc.

Here are some power packed insights from the research.[*#Note 2]

Most importantly, it also gave us a powerful insight into "WHAT type of messages, or ideas or incentives can backfire too when shared with a certain demographic of users" which helps us to understand core behind making BRAND monitoring an important aspect of any social media marketing campaign. At the end of the day, it is this 'connect' that helps your brand engage in real-time and have a relationship with your prospect or end user.

For eg. If we are using consumer insights and real-statistical data that helps us by understanding the target consumer better in the sense that, knowing in advance that a message for an Automobile advertisement that talks about "the vehicle's functionality" will connect with them quicker and more sincerely than suggesting to them about the "Economic affordability" or "Design uniqueness" of the said product in discussion, will then make the communication process so much more effortless. Plus, it then stays in their mind a lot longer as they automatically feel a 'connect' with their need from the said products appeal.

This is what we derived: What we have given below is highlights from our research:

Messages that appeal to consumers and end users on social media platforms:

- Incentives: The incentives offered by your product or service features finally determine how a particular message will be perceived by your audience. For eg. What appeals to a consumer buying a Television set, the same incentive will be ineffective to help you sell him a complete set of Book series or a two nights and three days stay at a premium resort. So the incentive and the tone in which your incentive is designed makes all the difference in making a prospect end up being a consumer of your said brand or product.

- Appeal: What appeals to users more? Many times, we feel that style, design or the aesthetics appeal to users, but more often than not, these same marketing messages are met with absolutely no impact whatsoever. Why does that happen? Our readers responses told us that certain types of product, even though rich in design and appeal, "appeals" to them more when their functionality is matched with "real-world usability of the said product" or "impact it derives in the minds of OTHERS while being associated with it".

- Instant gratification: It's often seen that offering discount or a freebie etc on the second purchase of a product or for referral etc works. But more often than not, an instant gratification appeals the best to a certain group of audiences. For eg. Offering an immediate Freebie with a "Fast food meal" is always an incentive to be a repeat customer at such places. Similarly, at times offering an instant freebie but with a condition that the same can be redeemed not immediately but only during the next visit mostly turns out to be a waste of time and efforts unless you offer that audience an option to do so within the comforts of their home.

- LISTEN to their opinions sincerely and respond: Users respond well when they realize that their ideas and opinions are being listened to. It might not have been put into practice by the said brand, but showcasing that their opinions have been sincerely given due importance, engages the users with the brand with a massively higher degree of brand loyalty and appeal. In other words, be sincere.

- Educate them and make a real value-add: Branding a financial services product or services across major social networking sites or using the broadcast medium does not always do the trick each time. Sometimes, it has been found that massive amounts of investment towards branding activities have gone completely fruitless. WHY? Well for starters, the moment you say "financial product or service" it's asking someone to TRUST you with their life savings or hard earned money. To make someone commit to such a trust requires remarkable request and a sincere message that says, "Yes, we are listening to you. We understand that your financial needs are very different from your next door neighbor or even your close friend and we can really add value to your future." Such messages when coupled with content that showcases real value-add for readers even when shared for free as an educating platform or blog etc that helps them with planning their investments, goals makes a long term impact in the minds of users.

- Humanize the brand: Move over the idea of merely branding and planning to "sell" your brand concepts. End readers and prospects connect with messages when they feel that they are engaging with "real people" and not just a company. At the end of the day, websites don't help you sell your brand products. People buy from people they trust. So it's extremely essential to humanize your brand. So let them talk to you, understand you better. Remember, it's not merely a sale, it's a RELATIONSHIP. Show happy emotions about a beautiful discovery or sports win, express grief as a human would over a tragic loss, but when you empower your brand with these powerful emotions, do so with utmost sincerity. It really reflects in your messages.

The toughest thing about the power of trust is that it's very difficult to build and very easy to destroy. The essence of trust building is to emphasize the similarities between you and the customer ~ Thomas J. Watson

- Time: Some people are very patient with tasks and some like things done quickly. Who are your end target customers? Make sure you understand very clearly who they are and what their response to "Time usage" is. For those users who are patient enough make sure to give them time to communicate and relate to your product and they will love it and for those who always feel that the clock is ticking, get their process as simplified as you can and you would have won their trust in your brand for ages.

- Branding or planning a CONTEST for your BRAND: Contests have been popular for quite some time now, especially online and off-late with the advent of power packed social sites like facebook and twitter, they are running every single day offering tons of freebies. But strangely enough though, most of these brands always end up complaining that neither did they see a surge in "purchases" during such contests, nor did their temporary "likes" or "follows" stay consistent even merely a week after the contest ended. So while integrating your campaign strategy with your brand, make sure, your contest would really appeal to your actual end prospects. For eg. Do you really believe that an individual hunting for an Armani suit would be busy browsing through social profiles for a discount offer or a freebie from the brand? No, most likely he would be more in tune with the brand if they offer better customization, comfort and a real essence of elegance to their products. Why? Because Armani today is more than just fashion, it's practically a way of life. And their end users know it.

Don't merely create a branding process or a branding strategy. Move beyond the term 'Branding' and let your end customers have a real relationship with your brand.

Have a wonderful connect ahead, for when you really connect with your consumers, you get long term brand ambassadors, friends and evangelists and the trust they build is sincere and truly priceless.

How safe is it to have an engaging relationship in real-time with end users online?

"Courteous treatment will make a customer a walking advertisement ~ James Cash Penney"

Consumers are KINGS. It's an adage so old and that has become such a cliché, especially with consumers themselves, that they have lost faith in it. Or at least, they had lost faith in it......then came the era of social media. Now this is an era where the power truly is with the consumers.

If you exist as a Brand, then someone out there is already talking about you. So make sure you are part of that conversation prism.

One cannot control or deny a consumer or an end user from writing reviews, comments etc, but yes, we can get into the metrics of "WHY" he/she has written that about you.

With more advanced tools and social media marketing process for eg. Our in-house 'Your SMQ® – Social media quotient' process with its analytic's and measuring metrics have evolved to empower our client brand partners to understand the WHY behind conversations online.

Gone is the era where a push marketing strategy or a pull marketing strategy was planned. In today's digital age the mediums and channels through which the marketing message is shared across the world works very differently.

Today a consumer or an end user has the power to become a GLOBAL BRAND Ambassador for your product with or without your approval.

It is as splendid as it is scary too, because he or she then inadvertently gets the power to speak your BRANDS tone out there in public. Pictures, videos and messages go viral in a pace that is unimaginable. For eg. PSY's Video crossed 44 Million views on YouTube in such a short span of time and made him a global super star helping him sell millions of his music records.

But does that mean, you can go and speak and or say anything when online. No, not really, in fact, with the power of social media and its blinding pace, it's extremely important to understand as a brand and listen to your own brand's tone and message online too.

Prior to engaging with your audiences, understand:

- Who is/are my end user(s)?
- Who really uses my product and can influence his or her group?
- How do I, as a BRAND, add more value to them?
- What content and which channel / medium would appeal for my product the most?

So you see, the questions above keep focusing on what the end consumer really needs. This will truly help you understand their pain areas without getting too personal.

The above questions takes us beyond the mere concept of "likes", "follows", "Views", "hits" and adds up valuable metrics in terms of REAL ROI on social media marketing. That is both measurable and re-usable with constant improvisation.

Draw a line as to what you, as a company or an organization or a brand will say or speak when online. Make sure to keep your corporate communication tone consistent throughout. Talk to them, listen carefully, take your time to understand their queries and respond to them accordingly. An eight to twelve hour time frame on social media is equal to almost a week's time in real-world time. So make sure to respond with speed and empathy to your social media users.

Trends: Should I be a part of the frenzy, just because everyone is talking about it?

Over the years, we as a digital marketing agency have generated high ROI on actual sales, ROI on Lead and high brand reach for our client brand partners across countries and industries by integrating a systematic social media marketing digital brand campaign that is both, well controlled and measurable.

Today, scores of brands have a tendency to tweet a picture or a marketing message of their brand, product, company or service and add it with a hashtag (#) that is among the most trending topics on twitter.

The idea being, hashtags are anyway trending so adding a hashtag to your messages with that hot topic or trend will reach users faster. Isn't that right?..... WRONG!

Trends are consumer driven as in they may be created by agencies or organizations, but to give it a boost of life, you need consumers to talk about it. Consumers and social media users speak and discuss hashtags and trends only when its truly personal for them. So forcibly adding a 'hot trend' or a top hashtag with your marketing message can even backfire on social media for you.

There are plenty of case studies wherein the greed to be a part of the trend frenzy has cost organizations millions and in some cases even billions of dollars with social media users blasting off the companies for misusing or misappropriating a phrase, keyword or a message.

There have been cases wherein company designed "trends" and 'hashtags' too have backfired because the companies boosting those trends merely did it for the cache they believed the key phrase could impact with online, but did not think it through of 'if' it backfires, then what?

So it's extremely important to make sure when you tweet with a hot topic or trend in mind, that message is completely in sync with your product, organization, brand or service at all times. Most importantly, with the emotional sentiments of users.

Also, at every stage, make sure to have a backup plan for your social media customer support to respond with utmost sincerity and empathy in case something goes wrong.

See image below to get an idea of some popular and negative 'trends' that have impacted conversations when online with social media users.

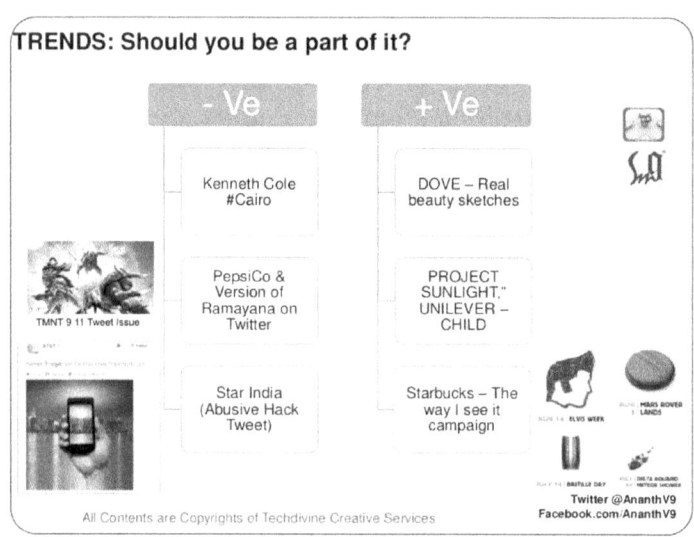

The image above represents popular cases of 'trend frenzy', some of which worked like a charm and some of it, well, you get the picture!

What do I track and how often do I measure my social media digital campaigns across my brand's varied marketing strategies?

Today, consumers have become more attached, loyal and aware of their emotional quotient towards brands and this is something, no corporate or brand can afford to ignore.

The process for every organizations social media marketing and brand monitoring campaigns should be integrated and in sync with Organizational vision, in-house & the digital marketing agency teams connect towards a common Goal for achieving optimum and realistic ROI. This will not only help you as a brand to grow, but also develop loyal real brand ambassadors for your brands.

(We have shared links to few of our case studies, at the end of this book, which have empowered brands using our social media marketing process to generate high and real-time ROI)

As an organization, always integrate your digital marketing campaigns with reports, analysis, consumer insights, brand goals and organizational ROI and track them every day. Also, have process that monitors your brand mentions across sites too.

What do I track?

Track what is relevant to you. Everything online can be quantified and measured. So make sure to do so?

How often do I measure?

Every single day. Your social media quality audit reports and consumer analytics with marketing research insights should be tracked everyday of your social media and digital marketing campaign.

What do I do with my company's traditional marketing strategies meanwhile?

Never sidetrack your traditional marketing campaigns. Make sure your marketing campaign, integrates both, your traditional marketing techniques and the new age media tools empowering your Content and brand message to end users.

This enables YOU as a BRAND to analyze, understand, design, plan, implement, MEASURE and improvise the campaign at every stage.

Make sure to give your end users a well planned, simple and easy to use platform where they can connect and engage with your brand on a real-time basis. At the end of the day, a successful social media or digital marketing campaign should enable you to bring together the offline and online users of your brands products and services under one single roof to engage with the brand.

Today, as a digital marketing agency we use and empower our social media quotient and brand marketing process in a manner in which it benefits both, the brands and end users as they are based on well planned and customized tools and strategies.

A simple way could be to use flyers, brochures and pamphlets of your organization and add QR codes, bar code scanner image and maybe even a geo-check in feature address which your users can interact with.

Let us now look into how to empower your brand's ROI by using:

ROI by using:

- SEO (Search engine optimization):
  How can SEO help you generate better ROI?
  SEO is search engine optimization. As a brand, if you are among the top pages on sites of search engines like Google, it's a brilliant start to your digital marketing campaign. Now, when I say, top pages, yes, I really mean only page numbers 1 and 2. Let's face it your prospects are not going to be spending time going beyond page no 2 on any search engine. So having a high ranking SEO score will definitely pace up your goals as a brand or an organization in terms of being visible and relevant to your end users queries online. Here again, we as a digital agency always stress to our brand partners to focus on both, online SEO and offsite but only with 'quality' searches with highest degree of product relevance. It's very important to note here that today, SEO goes way beyond websites. So SEO empowered via feeds and mentions across social networking sites like Google Plus, Facebook, Twitter, Instagram and blogging platforms play a massively important role today. The idea is to find a perfect balance between social networking sites, the content on your website and the impact of brand engagement across social media to converge into the right set of keywords and phrases for optimum SEO results.

  Let me share a real case study example of a B2B scenario. This is with respect to an industrial company for whom we were doing an SEO campaign (online and offsite).

The biggest concern the company had was, the keywords and phrases it needed us to focus on to increase its SEO were too generic, as in, they had over a million search results on Google and their website was ranking somewhere between page numbers 15 to 20 on search engines.

Their prime concern was to be on Google page No.1 for three to five keywords but at the same time, give their prospects a platform to reach out to them easily for queries too. Since their prospects were also corporate brands, they needed to keep the communication process as secure and private as possible, but at the same time user friendly to engage with.

We integrated blog, twitter and power tools with SEO for their organization and within the first three months, we delivered by getting them on Google Page No.1 and at the same time creating a social web platform in the form of a blog wherein their corporate prospect enquiries could easily drop in their queries and details while still being anonymous to other users online. This helped them safeguard their privacy too.

This was challenging because, as an agency, we never guarantee a GOOGLE Page no. 1 ranking, no one really can or even should, as it's based on hundreds of algorithms and process to validate tags, keywords, html, etc. I once had a very interesting meeting with one of the senior Google SEO experts during a Google event in India and interacting with such wonderful and brilliant professionals, truly gave me an amazing insight on the steps that we can take for our client websites to get them the best possible results using validated and approved process and strategies.

- Higher Brand reach:
  Higher brand reach is an obvious way to optimize your social media presence and focus on a higher ROI for your brand. With a higher brand reach the strategy that we always stress when on social media is 'think global and act local'. As a brand, reach out to a new section of demographics across countries but at the same time focus on core aspects of delivery, operations, logistics, sales, after-sales too while promoting your products and services online. Social media marketing does wonders for brands that are well known across a larger crowd and section of audiences as the trust factor is much higher with such brands and products. This is where, understanding the exact presence of your target customers plays a very vital role.

- Quality brand engagement:
  Many times we hear brands shouting out messages like "1 million followers", "15,000 fans", "5 million likes" etc but when you use the appropriate tools to measure those profiles "ACTUAL to SPAM or FAKE users Percentage" you realize that their quality of users engaging in reality with the brand is extremely low or poor. In certain cases, you might have even observed that, a page has around 60,000 likes but has less than 200 or 300 people actually interacting on a regular basis with the page. Most importantly, in social media marketing, having quality users engaging with your brand not only increases your brand sales, enquiries, leads, mentions etc but also adds up higher referrals across these social networking sites. Always remember, a quality brand user who engages with your product online is the best brand ambassador your organization can acquire.

Let me share another real case study example of a B2C scenario. One of our client brand partners was a restaurant in USA. The idea behind using social media marketing for their brand was to increase brand reach and at the same time generate more interest, footfalls into the restaurant. We kept sharing interesting content to engage more and more users and to increase their curiosity about the restaurant.

Our social media quotient process was in place too wherein we were monitoring some core keywords on social platforms like twitter, Google, facebook, foursquare etc. During one such campaign day, our social media team intercepted few core tags with positive emotions shared across social media and keyword phrases that they believed were related to our clients restaurant offerings. We reached out to the said user on twitter and had an engaging real-time conversation as she was traveling looking for a nice restaurant to eat at.

After we ensured that we were not being intrusive, but rather sincerely and empathetically listened to her food requirements for dinner that day, suggested a combination of starters and main course in a friendly way.

When we found her enquiring more details about the food, we even shared a picture with a Google map link to the easiest route to the said restaurant. Within an hour we got her tweet with her check-in dining at our client's restaurant. Not only that, she even tagged her friends with a tweet expressing how delicious her dinner was.

Now this is what I call, quality brand engagement and that too in real-time.

- Reaching target specific consumers:
  Metrics, metrics and more metrics. As a social media marketing agency, my company always advocates optimally using insights, marketing analytics, consumer research reports for every brands social media campaign. The best and easiest way to increase ROI for your brands management goals is by making appropriate use of your marketing insights to reach out to the consumers that are relevant and specific to your brand and products needs. For eg. Just because almost everyone across the globe is on facebook, does not mean your brand or product can sell or connect with the users on that platform too. For eg. Let's say your company deals with products and services that are sensitive in nature, like pharmaceutical or financial solutions etc. Very rarely consumers would like to engage with you on a public platform for such products. Understanding the metrics in your social media campaign, will help you plan the right platform which in turn will help you to give your TG (target group) an appropriate channel to reach out to you. This enhances ROI for your brand to a very great extent.

Here again, I am reminded of a case study for one of our clients wherein we used facebook insights, twitter metrics, Google analytics to focus on target specific customers for our client brand in the Retail industry to increase their store footfalls and enquiries. Within six months, we had increased their brand mentions by over 65%, their footfalls by 35% and their lead enquiries by 23%.

- Brand monitoring:
  You cannot control what others say about you, your brand, product and or services online. But that does not mean you don't need to be present online. As I quoted earlier, if you exist as a brand, someone out there is already talking about you. So do make sure you are part of that conversation prism too. Integrating brand monitoring helps to enhance your ROI in the most simple way, for eg. Positive mentions for your services will increase referrals, upgrades and negative mentions will help you turn an irate customer to a brand loyal ambassador when connected with on time online. Yes, there are plenty of tools online to do so, for eg, we have our own in-house Your SMQ Social media quotient process that focuses mainly on brand monitoring and social media quality metric reports.

- What to measure and how to measure it?
  Make sure not only the demographics of your users, but what social platforms are they most active on are also measured. Measure, plan, improvise, be patient and keep growing with team work and clear understanding of "how your customers are responding" online and what are their core real pain areas and how can YOU, as a BRAND, truly value-add with your product or services for them. Understand your brand's product influencer's online and empower them with the right incentives and instant gratification process.

  Further reading of this book will give you more detailed insights of the same.

ROI results sample report

ROI results across few industries & brands across countries
that we have worked with

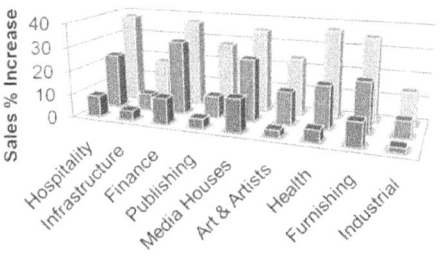

% Increase in Sales

- Sales without SMM
- Sales with SMM
- Sales with SMM & Metrics

INDUSTRIES

Shows Percentage increase in Leads/Sales & Conversions

<u>Best and worst times to post on social networking sites</u>

- On Facebook:
    - o Best time: 1 pm - 4 pm
    - o Worst time: 8 pm – 8 am
- On Twitter:
    - o Best time: 1 pm - 3 pm
    - o Worst time: 8 pm – 8 am
- On Google plus:
    - o Best time: 9 am – 11 am
    - o Worst time: 7 pm – 7 am
- On Pinterest:
    - o Best time: 2 pm – 4 pm and during 8 pm – 12 am
    - o Worst time: 5 pm to 7 am
- On Blog:
    - o Best time: 11 am
    - o Worst time: 11 pm - 8 am
- On LinkedIn:
    - o Best time: 7 am - 9 am & during 5 pm to 6pm
    - o Worst time: 10 am to 6 pm

Though the above timings have stood the test of time for us across brands based on our experiences over the years, I would like to point out that this will not work particularly if you are catering to consumers across different countries simultaneously. For eg. If I need to cater to consumers in India and USA, then posting at 10 am in India will share the content across the same page for users in USA during 10 pm. So the idea here is to have different strategies while posting to users across countries using the same profile page on social networking sites while online.

Sales conversions and social media ROI

Let us first understand few terminologies:

LTV, CPC and CAC are few terms that we use frequently while integrating and measuring Social media ROI using our in-house "Your SMQ® – social media quotient' process.

- LTV – Lifetime value of a customer
- CPC – Cost per customer
- CAC – Customer acquisition cost
- Your SMQ® – Social media quotient

Let us look at different scenarios in which we measure them:

Scenario 1: For eg, an LTV is the lifetime value of a customer. Let's say for a simple understanding, each customer generates revenue of Rs.100 on an average in his or her lifetime. On an average 1 in every 10 visitors to your blog register for a product or service as a customer, then the LTV is 100/10 i.e. Rs.10/-

Scenario 2: CPC i.e. cost per customer which goes beyond the LTV. It would include the average cost of resources and time taken to acquire a lead and to convert a lead to an actual sale.

For eg. In case you have spent on an average of Rs.10,000/- per month (SMM) in which you have generated 100 leads of which 10 leads were finally converted to sales. Each customer generates revenue of Rs.1,000/- (R) in his or her lifetime, you would need to calculate the (CPC) cost per customer or the (CAC) customer acquisition cost as under:

CAC or CPC = SMM / R = 10,000 / 1,000 = Rs.10/-

Scenario 3: Your SMQ® – Social media quotient - This is a Registered brand under our company under which we measure multiple in-depth reports that include analytics of:

- Consumer research
- SEO & Adwords optimization
- Integration of Google analytics into the report
- Leads / enquiry
- Referrals
- SMM
- SMM Ads (Paid reach)
- Website Redirects / Pingbacks (Paid)
- Branding & PR online
- Email subscriber conversions & so much more.......

In the above case of 'Your SMQ®', the process is much more detailed and more precise as it includes and takes into consideration cost factors such as time, process, human resources, actual SEO conversions, fall back enquiries, referrals, mentions and pingbacks referrals for leads, actual sales conversions etc.

As a brand make sure to integrate process that brings together insights, reports, analytics across landing pages, email marketing, SEO, adwords, social media paid ads, website referral ads etc.

Today, users are researching across groups, posts on blogs, facebook, twitter links, Google plus communities etc to learn, understand and be aware of the products, pricing and services across industries with real-time feedback and reviews about the products and services from friends and peers online.

So it's extremely essential to make sure there is a proper tool and process in place to measure your ROI in real-time.

(At the end of this book, I have shared few links and ways to reach us in case you would like to know more about the process and tools to measure in-depth ROI for your social media marketing campaign)

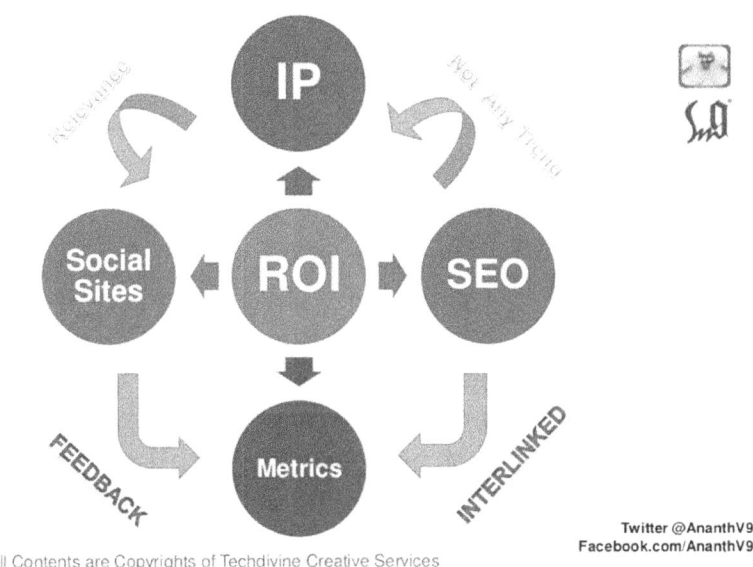

General Skeleton of tracking Social media ROI

Twitter @AnanthV9
Facebook.com/AnanthV9

"Why would users online engage with YOUR BRAND on SOCIAL MEDIA?"

<u>Research across 1,000 users engaging with social networking brand pages across the following industries:</u>

- Hotels and hospitality
- Movies
- Real-estate
- Retail
- Finance & banking solutions
- Publishing
- IT institutes
- Management institutes and
- Trading & Broking

for their valuable insights based on industry specific brand pages across social networking sites on:

- Time spent on social networking sites and time spent interacting with brand pages
- Which social networking sites do you use the most?
- Referrals, re-sell, upgrade & brand loyalty: How and what makes them BUY?
- Why would you engage with a brand?

"What can you as a BRAND, acquire or get from this survey?"

- Know about the 'Most effective social tactics or strategy and platforms to engage users online'
- Understand 'What matters to users online the most while engaging with a brand'
- Find out 'Which social networking sites are most users active on?'
- Find out 'How much time do they spend online and how much of that time they spend engaging with brand pages?'

<u>Highlights from the survey with Consumers</u>

- Percentage of users surveyed across each industry
- Time spent online and with brand pages / profiles
- Which social networking sites do you use most?
- Referrals, re-sell, upgrade & brand loyalty: How and what makes them BUY?
- Why would you engage with a brand

Percentage of users surveyed across nine industries:

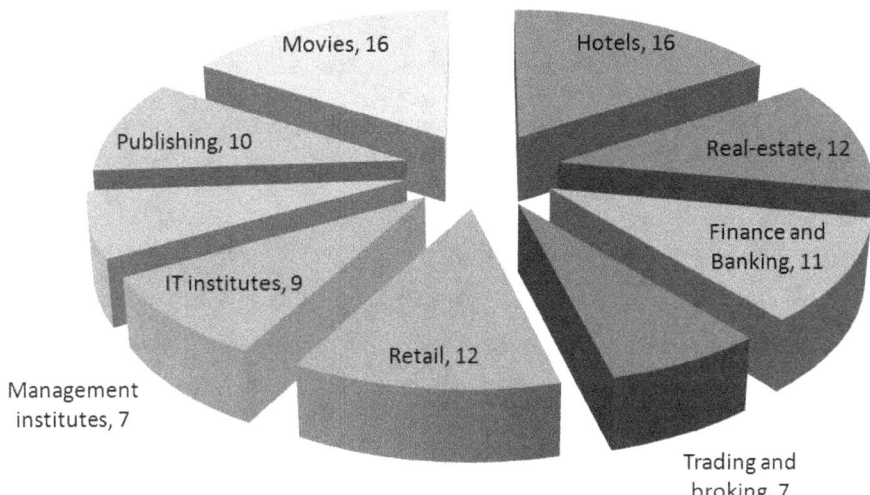

From the total of 1,000 users: They were fans and followers of pages, brand profiles and products from:
- Hotels and hospitality 16%
- Movies 16%
- Real-estate 12%
- Retail 12%
- Finance & banking solutions 11%
- Publishing 10%
- IT institutes 9%
- Management institutes 7%
- Trading & Broking 7%.

Time spent online and with brand pages / profiles: (How much time do they spend online and how much of that time they spend engaging with brand pages?)

Hours Spent Online across social sites & brand pages

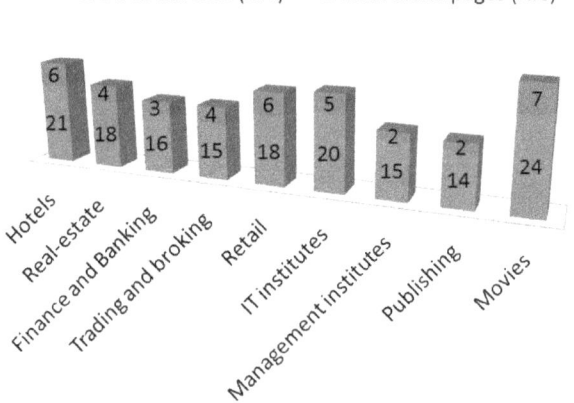

Indicates Hours spent by users Online PER WEEK on Social networking sites and at the same time hours they spend PER WEEK across Brand pages during those visits online.

On an average each user is spending around 2-3 hours per day and around 14 – 24 hours in all per week across social networking sites. During these visits, the time they actually spend PER WEEK engaging with brand pages (multiple brand pages across different sites) is around 2 to 7 hours in a week's time.

Now these are visits and time spent by them across various brand pages and across multiple social networking sites when online.

So as a marketer, it is very essential to share content that is both valuable and resourceful to keep them engaged with your brand.

Which social networking sites do you use the most: (Which social networking sites are most users active on?)

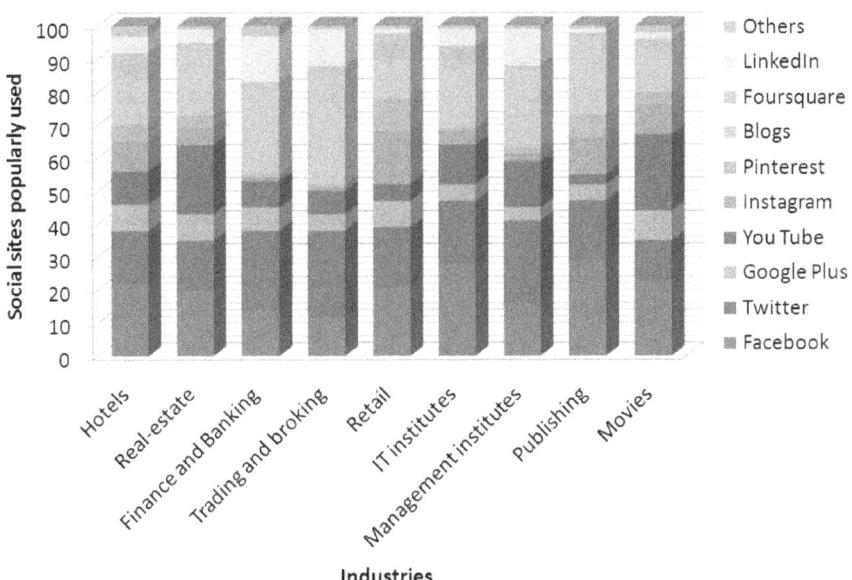

Most popular platforms used by consumers across social and related sites online for the above mentioned industries are as under:

Facebook, Twitter, Blogs and You Tube followed by Google plus, Instagram, LinkedIn, Pinterest, Foursquare and others (Sites like Myspace, Etsy, iOS apps, Android apps etc).

Referrals, re-sell, upgrade & brand loyalty: How and what makes them BUY? (Most effective social tactics or strategy and platforms)

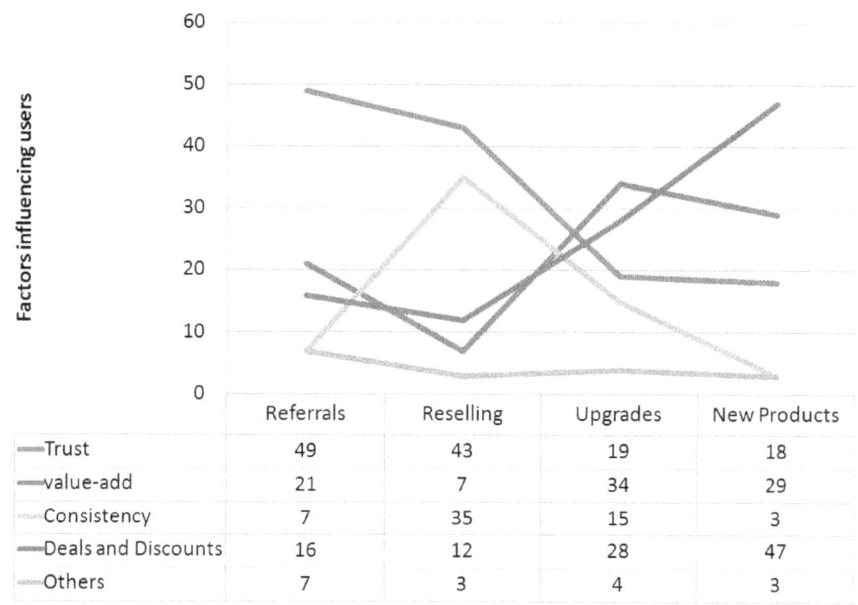

	Referrals	Reselling	Upgrades	New Products
Trust	49	43	19	18
value-add	21	7	34	29
Consistency	7	35	15	3
Deals and Discounts	16	12	28	47
Others	7	3	4	3

Top factors that influenced users to purchase products online:

In case of '**Referrals**', their **TRUST** factor mattered the most, whereas in case of '**New products**', **DEALS & DISCOUNTS** offered online mattered the most.

It is also interesting to note that for **Reselling** products to the same users, consumers engaging on social platforms preferred to rate '**consistency**' in terms of brand engagement, product quality experience the highest whereas in the case of **upgrades**, they voted highest for **value-adds** and **deals and discounts** from brands.

Why would you engage with a brand: (What matters to users online the most while engaging with a brand?)

% of Users: Why would they prefer to engage with your BRAND on social platforms?

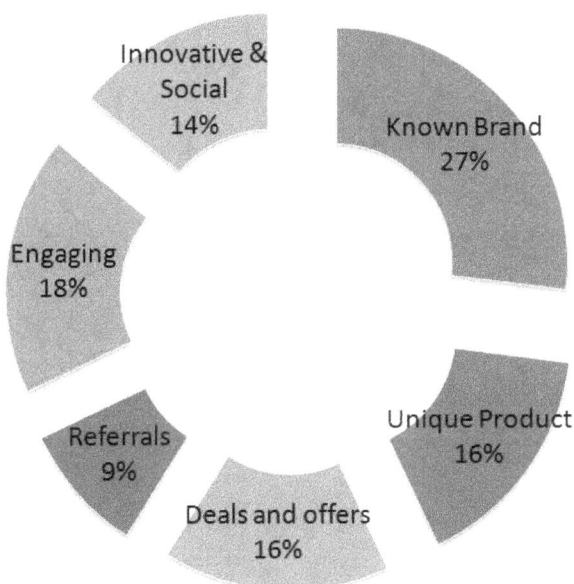

Majority of the users said they would 'like' or 'follow' a brand on social networking sites if they already were familiar with the brand name. This response was interestingly followed by users, voting for 'brands that were *engaging* online' as in, easy to connect with, interesting to talk to and fun to read their updates etc. In this case, they voted for 'human quality' while engaging and responding the highest rather than automated process and tools to do the same. Qualities like empathy, listening to their feedback and responses and giving replies based on the same, responding professionally rather than in a very informal tone or in an over-friendly manner etc made the most impact.

It is very interesting to note here that users voted 'brand engagement', 'ease to interact with the brand' as a factor more important than 'deals and discounts' as a reason to connect with a brand on social media.

This clearly showcases the importance users place on 'humanized brand relationships' especially across social networking sites.

BONUS CONTENT:

Bonus content features our top five social media and digital marketing posts from our company's corporate blog posts over the years that have received the best responses and are still relevant: The posts have been edited for meeting today's tool and new age media process:

- Misconceptions about social media
- Creative story telling using social media
- Power SEO Tips for your website
- Key branding rules when online
- Don't make a social faux pas

Bonus content:

1. Misconceptions About Social Media

a) Social media is free marketing: "Nothing is free unless you buy the giant size first" goes the adage in advertising and marketing.

It's especially true in the case of social media marketing simply because the primary tool it requires are resources in the form of professionals, experts in their respective fields of design, development, marketing, branding, strategy design & of course programming.

The general belief is that, when all these social networking sites are free and when even a teenage kid can create a facebook page on it, why does it have to be a "paid" medium? Well, the answer is quite simple.

Would you want your teenage kid to run your BRAND campaigns?

We are guessing your answer is NO.

This is why it's always better to make sure such digital marketing campaigns are only handled by professionals.

b. You can't measure your return on investment in social media: Social media ROI is very much measurable provided, one defines the right goals and metrics, and if your data collection system works well, then there is no reason why your campaign should not work.

c. Social media can replace your website: It's important to understand that social media is an additional tool and process to help you nurture your brand and to connect with a wide range of prospects globally. The idea is not to replace your website, at least definitely not at this stage.

d. Blogging is a waste of time: Voicing your opinion and that too with a personalized connect can never be a waste of time. That's what a BLOG does. It gives you the edge that a website does not. It helps you "humanize your brand".

e. Social media is 'just' a fad: If we turn time by merely few decades, we can recollect people believing "Internet is a fad". Well we all know now how internet has changed and become an integral part of our life today. Likewise, with the increasing number of mobile phones with smart technology, tablets all ensure a diverse base for social media platforms in the near future. Well, frankly speaking, aren't majority of us already online all the time!

f. Social Media is not for my type of businesses: It's a myth that social media can work for customer oriented model of business only. It works well even for the B2B model of business.

g. Buy your Fans/Followers, there is nothing wrong in that, or is it?: It's a myth that more the number of followers would mean more the number of customers. It's important to remember that such paid fans are not real fans, most of the time. So it's best for business to have organic and real fans rather than you ending up having a bunch of ghost profiles on your page that do not interact with your brand. We are not suggesting that you do not go for paid ads, no, but buying "fake" profiles or "fake" followers is a strict No!

h. Social Media is all about Me, me and ME: As Bill Stinnett correctly says "Think like your customer". It's important to ask this simple question to oneself "Do I like having a conversation with someone who is constantly talking about himself?" Of course you don't. That's how customers will feel about your company if you're constantly pushing a marketing message through social media. The conversations should engage the customers and make them talk about your brand. Remember, it's "social" media. Be real, talk, listen and engage. It reflects in your brand's personality online.

i. Social Media is just Facebook and Twitter: Facebook is a wonderful medium for social media marketing. But remember, "Social media is not about websites. It was, is and will always be about people. People buy from people they trust. So make sure in your engagement and conversations, you humanize your brand". Focus on your goals, customer's needs and their presence online.

j. Our customers aren't on social sites: It is true that social media was at one time an arena dominated by young adults and teenagers. Not only are people using social networks to connect with family and friends of all age groups, but they are using them for opinions, news, feedback, deals and offers and that too for extended periods of time. People spend an average of 5.1 hours per day on social networks. That is more time they spend on email, news, games, or anything else on the Internet. Which is why, first understanding where your customers are plays a very vital role in planning your social media campaign.

k. Remove traditional marketing: We say NO. Never replace traditional marketing, at least not at the stage right now where the world is not completely ready across the globe to go digital. The best solution is to find a way to bring together your online and offline consumers under one banner to engage with your brand. Get them both working together and leverage on each of their strengths.

l. Brand monitoring, spam posts and irate customers: Social media will backfire: This is another huge misconception or fear that is there among many end users that, social media can backfire anytime and there is nothing one can do about it. Also, that when 'customers go irate on social media, shut them down or delete their comments or block them' is another misconception users have about social media which needs to radically change.

Are there any other queries or misconceptions that you might have heard anyone share with you about social media or digital marketing? Feel free to share your feedback and comments with me on my social profile site links shared at the end of this book.

Bonus content:

2. <u>Creative story telling using social media:</u>

Social media as a marketing and branding platform for brand managers, professional marketers and the new age entrepreneurs today, goes beyond "likes" or "follows". Social media for such business professionals, such as CEO's and stakeholders is a "power packed marketing, branding, sales conversion & PR tool". But most importantly, these business leaders know, that it is an amazing tool which when planned, designed and monitored well, can harness the power of storytelling in a way that connects with consumers and prospects in real-time and most importantly, in a very personal manner. It helps them leverage the BRAND reach, value and boosts them to 'humanize the brand'

Story telling using social media means to share the insights of the product, value of the brand, concept behind creating the said service and so much more, but doing so creatively, so as to engage users to interact with the brand.

It's very obvious that in today's digital world its vital for every business and Organization to have its presence on digital and social media platform. When we say social media, we are not merely referring to the posts on Facebook, tweets or trends on Twitter or for that reason just another blog post. We are talking about the complete 360 degree social media process by ways of which one can plan, design, implement and measure the return on the investment as well.

To start with the story telling process, it's important for companies to have well defined and specific goals.

Goals like increase in leads/ enquiries by 15% in first quarter, or increase in footfalls by 65% etc. depending on company's requirement.

Identify your target audience and accordingly choose a social media platform or channels for marketing. Set timelines and deadlines in line with your goals. Plan a strategy based on the same and implement and review those strategies. Reinforce the ones that work the best.

Empowering appropriate social networking sites in connect with your target market industry and taking into consideration the fact that your prospects are comfortable interacting with the said channel and platform is when the process of storytelling using social media begins. But what happens when you add the power of Metrics. Your social media brand marketing campaign goes beyond mere follows, likes and favorites. It touches astonishing figures when the right metrics are measured and the consistency is seen while engaging users with creative story telling about the brand, products and services.

I am yet again reminded of this power quote from Peter Drucker "The purpose of a business is to create a customer."

So let us look at the said quote from today's point of view. Let's keep in mind that when we talk about brands and consumers today, we are talking about their mindset, their behavioral pattern, their loyalty towards our company products or services etc.

Let's truly understand the customer's needs and requirement and here again, well planned and strategic social media marketing can be a powerful tool in the aspect of consumer metrics.

This, when coupled with engaging story telling process using social media, makes the experience worthwhile for the end users too.

Have you ever wondered why the truly big and successful companies or brands have achieved so much success in creating an impact on customers mind? This is majorly because of the "Trust" that they have been able to build. For eg. When an icon and industry leader like Ratan Tata says "We never compromise on ethics" what rings in our mind is the "trust factor." In fact, the moment we hear the word ethics in industry or trust in the corporate world, the first word that comes to our mind today is TATA. Why, because they have been truly able to "Humanize the brand" not by merely sharing services and products, but with really connecting with the end users.

First, we strongly believe that the consumer needs to be made aware of what that product can really do for him / her and a real social media marketing campaign, involves the end users as part of the brand conversations too. But yes, in a well monitored way. Gartner research had shared that they expect global business intelligence (BI) software to pass $17 billion in 2016, more than $4 billion higher than in 2013. What does that tell you? That metrics in a digital media is as important as your Brand goals too.

So make sure, you integrate ROI for Social media campaign for your brand as a key aspect for your SMM results and business goals.

In today's world, we have the power to leverage this aspect with creative story telling using social media marketing. Look at how OREO is in sync with BRAND storytelling and trends at every stage across every site online.

Creative story telling means something the consumers are inclined to read, something that they are looking forward to or they need to know. It simply follows the principle of "Give and take." One must follow the simple steps to creative writing -

- Listen, join, engage and share content that is of real value.
- Its human nature to relate to something faster when you are able to engage with the brand and know about the product/ services offered, in terms of information from more than what is already offered in their advertisement or brochure.

Let's look at an example here. Suppose you are looking to invest in Mutual funds but you do not have enough information to truly go ahead and make the decision to invest in it. Then you go online and search for information and in this process you come across a site with all related details of mutual fund and they even help you in real-time with your FAQ's. Wouldn't you then be more comfortable in investing with such a firm? Of course you will. Why? Not because it gave you all the information you are looking for, but more so because it was not 'sold' to you. You found resourceful content presented to you in a simplified manner and most importantly, you found help to connect to in real-time. Now, it's obviously not as simple as it sounds, but you get the idea right?

Thus creating this kind of simplified reach, real-time connect and impact requires professional help and preferably a team of individuals who are experts in this process. Now make sure you do not fall for the "FREE Social media campaign or CHEAP LIKES and FOLLOWS with social media" by any company or professional.

Remember, it's your BRAND at stake here. Make sure you hand over the social media campaign to an agency or business who understands what YOU need and who have showcased similar results across industries over the years.

A smart and growing business and brand today will make sure that their marketing and sales team is integrating the appropriate social media tools and process to get the best results for their customized business goals.

Bonus content:

3. Power SEO:
   Few simple steps to a clean, light and content rich searchable website:
   - Keep it light: Make sure the web pages are light in file size. Use more of images which are compressed format's optimized for web.
   - Tag your HTML properly: Use right formats of HTML and validate them. More than flash files, html pages can be indexed quicker and faster.
   - Headline and Title: Make sure your website does not have too many repetitive headline or title tags throughout the website. Many search engines may read this as spam texts rather than keywords.
   - Core Keywords: Make sure each webpage uses maximum of one or two keywords across the webpage and not too many. It helps in ascertaining the right tag to pull for the particular page which they are being indexed or searched.
   - Proper Name for URL: Do not use numbered names in Uniform resource locators (URL) of your website. For eg. If your main page is going to talk about chocolates, make sure your page name is something like chocolate.html or choco.html etc and not ch12.html.
   - Text or images: Search engines indexes the pages based on textual content. So keep fewer images and more of text. But make sure the text is not repetitive in nature.
   - Alt Text your Images: When using images, do not randomly name them. Add "alt text" tags to images with captions if possible and make sure the name of the image does justice to the subject of the image. For eg. If the subject for the page is a motivational quote and the

picture is of a rising sun, naming it 'motivate' would make more sense than sunrise.

- When in Rome, be a Roman: Be a part of the discussions across similar websites like that of yours or forums or groups which discuss products and services that you offer. It takes care of your Off-page SEO for you too.

- As you sow, shall you reap: Back links and pingbacks: Make sure you offer websites to redirect or pingback to you based purely on their content and not just on their page ranks. Many a times you might get those "tempting" offers for website pingbacks from spamming sites too, avoid them at all costs. Also, add links to sites from your site or blog to those sites which are high on quality page ranking by search engines.

- Keep them alive: Make sure you check your site for broken links and proper navigation across pages.

- Add a sitemap if you can for your website too.

Bonus content:

4. <u>Key branding rules when online:</u>

Brand managers today have been placed at a position, more accountable than ever before.

So it is very much essential to know the key BRANDING rules to follow especially on an online platform.

<u>'Key' rules:</u>

- For implementing BRAND Campaigns online, the core needs to be always on the Brand goals and not the sites or tools for implementing it. Content is king, create value for end users and deliver it keeping in mind your goals.

- Responsibly use the available platforms after properly analyzing them and understand clearly the technology available through those online social networking site platforms before placing your brand on it.

- What to post when: Time your content posting based on metrics and reports that help you plan the same for optimum reach.

- Always add a face to your voice, whatever be the platform you are using. Let people know, who they are interacting with. Humanize your brand.

- Integrate your multiple platforms together and stay in sync with the content that you promise to share and actually end up sharing. Remember, once your promises are Online, your products, services, reputation is on-the-line too.

- Most importantly, understand that the platform is not to "sell" but to connect. Engagement and relationship with the end users is the key here.

- Privacy, content, IP's are to be clearly showcased across platforms. Reusing of your content, selling it for commercial and such other interests of third parties should be made very clear about.

- Better safe than sorry. Always understand that what is once online, stays online. So make sure, the information you are showcasing online, is something that you can afford to be shared by all those you know and those you don't and all that, in just a matter of seconds. So it's very essential to make sure you add disclaimers, adherence guides etc to your content.

- There needs to be a sense of great responsibility too. Make sure your team working across online campaigns understands and implements the right tone and message that your Organization has built over the years as part of your campaign.

- Respond: Whatever may be the conversation happening around you, about your brand or organization, respond positively. In case of any dissatisfaction expressed about your product or service respond with utmost sincerity and get to the root cause behind complains at the earliest. Address it and provide proper responses unless the feedback or comments are repetitive by an individual whose nature and online characteristic seems to be disruptive and destructive in general.

Make sure, you learn to ignore and at the same time create a back-end system to resolve an intentional and unwanted negative comment or feedback from a user online. Remember, you cannot change people, you can only channel them your way.

- Your in-house team and any agency that's part of the campaign and working together, need to work towards the campaign with the common goal of 'elevating the brand' and not each other's skills or tools. If that is the case, then neither of them has remotely understood the idea behind social campaigns. As an organization, it is your duty too to make sure that your in-house marketing team and your third party agency are in sync and complement each other and not compete with each other. At the end of the day, it's your BRAND!

- Do not share personal information, especially of clients and members online under any circumstances. Always keep your member groups moderated in terms of the content being posted.

- Bottom-line: If you exist online or offline as a BRAND, there's someone out there always talking about you. Be a part of the conversation prism.

Bonus content:

5. <u>Don't make a social faux pas: Get your Netiquettes right when online across social media sites:</u>

Quite often, many users commit online faux pas' which they come to regret later. We have tried to list a few such online faux pas which you might have come across when you are browsing various social sites.

a. Most important of all, do not share your personal details online. Never give out your address, phone number, credit card details or other information if you are not sure about the credibility of the party on the other end.

b. Please change your password at least once every two or three months.

c. Think twice before sharing pictures ridiculing others on social networking sites. It may seem like a cool thing to post or in internet jargon, an LOL image, but do take a moment to consider whether it makes fun of a sensitive topic. While humor is good, it should not be at the expense of others. Also keep in mind that you might have a few minors in your social circle (even though officially you have to be 18 to sign up) and you would not want them to see such images.

d. Do not post personal comments on official or brand pages. For eg: Someone you know might have an official brand page. Don't make informal comments on the page. Communicate through some other channel. You don't want to embarrass the other person.

e. If you are tagging a person, make sure the tag is relevant. People do not appreciate being spammed with irrelevant tags. If you do have to bring their attention to an album, tag them in one of the photos instead of in each & every one of them.

f. Don't get into flame wars with others on your profile. Do not respond with abuses to any insults thrown at you. Rather avoid commenting on that topic. This preserves your integrity without sullying your name.

g. Don't let your posts be only about you all the time. Be social & keep engaging with others. Everybody likes a pat on the back. Remember it's a "social site" at the end of the day.

h. Make sure you customize your privacy settings such that your personal data or photos are shared only with those who matter instead of everyone in your friends list.

i. While protecting your personal data, also make sure not to share other individuals' private information under any circumstances.

j. If you have added your boss, teacher or any other senior to your friends, refrain from making any derogatory comments about them.

At the end of the day always remember, if you are online someone somewhere is always watching you. Keep it clean and have a wonderful connect online.

Test your SOCIAL MEDIA BRAND quotient.

The questions are based on this book and here is how you could **WIN** the surprise from me to You!

What is the SURPRISE that you could WIN?

Follow the process given below and you could win a spot as a GUEST AUTHOR*** on our professional and extremely well reputed Corporate Social media marketing blog that has hosted online PR campaigns, review and blog posts of some high profile brands over the past several years. Moreover, once approved your post goes live across our social networking sites online too.

As a GUEST AUTHOR you could win an opportunity to be featured with your –

- Name and Photograph
- Profile bio
- Designation
- Academic and other credentials
- Your company and brand bio with link url to Facebook, Website, Twitter pages
- Guest article post with not more than 900 words with spaces and two images in jpeg format.
- Once approved, your post goes live from our end and gets shared across our social networking sites online throughout the month.

*** Conditions apply: The conditions for winning the position on our reputed blog as a GUEST AUTHOR are given in detail below. Don't worry they are quite simple, very easy to follow and straightforward. But do go through the same to know the rules, guidelines etc.

How to give the test:

- Go through the questions below from Q1 to Q20 and note down your answers in a notepad or a notebook.
- Once you have completed the test, scroll down further in this book to check out the answers.
- Compare, verify and calculate your score with the answers given in this book
- Every right answer gets 10 points.

Do this for a chance to WIN, if you get a score of 100 points or more:

Follow me on Twitter @AnanthV9 and drop me a tweet (https://www.twitter.com/AnanthV9) as under:

@AnanthV9 Social media marketing brand quotient quiz #AnanthV #Socialmedia #Book "Your SCORE"

And / OR

You can like my page on Facebook (https://www.facebook.com/AnanthV9) and post on my Facebook page profile (https://www.facebook.com/AnanthV9) as under:

My Social media marketing brand quotient quiz book score is "Your Score"

Social media marketing brand quotient QUIZ questions:

Q1. Social media quotient is your company's _____ when online.

Q2. Every campaign of social media is measurable, so have clearly defined _____.

Q3. Set _____ that are realistic.

Q4. Social media is not about websites. It was, is and will always be about people. People buy from people they trust, so _____ your BRAND.

Q5. It is never merely _____ which appeals to users, but the process within that helps them actually converse with the brand on a personal level.

Q6. The _____ offered by your product or service features finally determine how a particular message will be perceived by your audience.

Q7. Remember, it's not merely a sale, it's a _____.

Q8. _____ today is more than just fashion, it's practically a way of life

Q9. When you really connect with your consumers, you get long term brand ambassadors, friends and evangelists and the trust they build is _____ and truly priceless.

Q10. Consumers are _____.

Q11. If you exist as a Brand, then someone out there is for sure already talking about you. So make sure you are part of that conversation _____.

Q12. How do I, as a BRAND, add more _____ to them?

Q13. Make sure to keep your _____ communication tone consistent throughout.

Q14. _____: Should I be a part of the frenzy, just because everyone is talking about it?

Q15. Have process that monitors your _____ mentions across sites too.

Q16. A simple way could be to use flyers, brochures and pamphlets of your organization and add _____ codes

Q17. _____ empowered via feeds and mentions across social networking sites like Google Plus, Facebook, Twitter, Instagram and blogging platforms play a massively important role today.

Q18. In social media marketing, having quality users engaging with your brand not only increases your brand sales, enquiries, leads, mentions etc but also adds up higher _____ across these social networking sites.

Q19. LTV stands for _____ _____ of a customer.

Q20. Your SMQ® stands for another registered brand of our company named Your _____ _____ _____.

Some core HIGHLIGHTS from the book: GIST:

- Make sure of not only the demographics of your users, but what social platforms are they most active on.
- Make it simple and easy for your customers and prospects to engage with your brand.
- Measure, plan, improvise, be patient and keep growing with team work and clear understanding of "how your customers are responding" online and what are their core real pain areas and how can YOU, as a BRAND value-add with your product or services to them.
- Understand your brand and product influencer's online
- Empower data and brand monitoring analysis
- Make sure your in-house team and or your digital agency are in sync and working together with equal faith in the process. Faith & loyalty brand building, always starts in-house.
- Have complete brand monitoring and corporate communication control over your social media marketing and brand process online at every stage of the campaign.
- Social media marketing is not about websites. It was, is and will always be about people. People buy from people they trust. So humanize your brand.
- If you exist as a brand, someone out there is already talking about you. Make sure you are part of the conversation prism.
- Today, it's as important to listen to your own brand's voice and tone online as it is to listen to your consumers and competitors.
- Brands today have a much more responsible role than ever before, i.e. to connect with the consumer within.
- Always make sure to integrate measurable metrics with your digital marketing campaign.

- LTV, CAC, CPC and Your SMQ Social media quotient are metrics and process from our end that will empower you to measure real-time ROI for both, brands and end users.

ANSWERS to Social media marketing brand quotient QUIZ

Ans 1. measurable metric.

Ans 2. Goals

Ans 3. Timelines

Ans 4. Humanize

Ans 5. BRANDING

Ans 6. incentives

Ans 7. RELATIONSHIP

Ans 8. Armani

Ans 9. sincere

Ans 10. KINGS

Ans 11. prism

Ans 12. value

Ans 13. corporate

Ans 14. Trends

Ans 15. brand

Ans 16. QR

Ans 17. SEO

Ans 18. referrals

Ans 19. Lifetime value

Ans 20. Social media quotient

If your score total is above 100 points do tweet me or post on my facebook profile link as mentioned below for a chance to win an opportunity to be a GUEST AUTHOR on our corporate social media marketing blog.

CONDITIONS of the QUIZ:

1. Follow me on Twitter @AnanthV9
   (https://www.twitter.com/AnanthV9) AND OR
2. Like my page on Facebook
   (https://www.facebook.com/AnanthV9)
3. Tweet to me as under –

@AnanthV9 Social media marketing brand quotient quiz #AnanthV #Socialmedia #Book "Your SCORE"

OR you can also choose to Post on my Facebook profile link given above as -

My Social media marketing brand quotient quiz book score is "Your Score"

4. There will be a maximum of 5 Guest Post WINNERS.
5. Our decision to select the winners, approving, responding to the tweets or posts and any and all decisions thereto with respect to the quiz will be final and not debatable under any circumstances.
6. Even after an individual is selected, the decision to approve his or her post, content, links, sharing it if at all any and approving media images or video links thereto in the said post will be our final decision and not questionable under any circumstances including the time duration to do so.
7. Winners once selected to be guest authors will need to abide by our rules and guidelines with respect to the article post prior to submitting to us for consideration

to be made live across our sites as deemed suitable from our end.

Personal note: I would love to see your blog post go live on our corporate blog, but we have added the above conditions just to make sure the content is appropriate, completely approved, originally written by the author claiming to have sent it to us, has no content in the post that is inappropriate for any audience or to make sure it does not have any content deemed offensive or to impact negatively on any religious, political sentiments of any of our readers across countries and demographics.

Hope you found this book resourceful.

I am eagerly looking forward to your feedback and comments.

You can share your review of this book here on Amazon and also write and connect with me across these sites online -

Twitter @AnanthV9 (https://www.twitter.com/AnanthV9)
Facebook @AnanthV9 (
https://www.facebook.com/AnanthV9)
LinkedIn (http://in.linkedin.com/in/techdivine)
My personal blog - (http://ananthv9.wordpress.com)

NOTES:

*Note 1 Social media quotient: In case you would like us to measure the social media quotient for your corporate brand or your brand's products and services, feel free to reach our team at socialmedia@techdivine.com or reach me directly across social sites on Twitter @AnanthV9 or www.facebook.com/AnanthV9

*##Note 2 Interested in getting our complete research insights, contact us for more information with the SUBJECT line "Research Techdivine" – socialmedia@techdivine.com

**#Note 3 You can read more about our revolutionary marketing and social media process on our slideshare presentation: Link here: http://www.slideshare.net/YourSMQ/social-media-marketing-revolutionary-process-from-techdivine

Few useful resources, links and case studies:

- GOOGLE business group Live presentation Highlights with pictures TOPIC: "ROI on social media for BRANDS by Ananthanarayanan V in Mumbai - www.techdivine.com/tdblog/2013/12/google-business-group-mumbai-event-pictures-and-highlights

- Direct PDF link to CASE STUDY – ROI on actual sales using our social media marketing process – http://goo.gl/NtWlzq

- Case study 2 link - http://www.techdivine.com/tdblog/2012/08/delivering-brand-goals-with-social-media-marketing-read-case-studies

Source:
Techdivine Creative Services - www.techdivine.com

Important guidelines for using this book:

This book has been written by me using the experience gained across brands and industries over the years and with the various case study experiences that we have as an agency built, designed and implemented for our client brand partners. Every social media and digital marketing campaign has been customized with us. All contents, process and case studies shared in this book are copyrights of Techdivine Creative Services and cannot be reproduced for commercial or other purposes without written approval from me.

It is important to note that, while this book will definitely add tremendous value to your already rich expertise and experience in the field of digital marketing, the process given should not be duplicated for your brands or clients. Reason being, each industry, brand, products and their end users at every stage have a different response process. Due to which it is always advisable to make sure that the research insights you have about your target customers is most recent and relevant.

There are various factors like customer research insights, relevant content, innovative process and tools etc that go into designing, developing and implementing a social media campaign or any digital marketing campaign.

We will not be held responsible for any idea, process or inference that is derived from you and or your team after reading this book. This book is written with an idea of creating a knowledge resource wherein my experiences across industries and by our team has been put together to explain the intense and meticulous process that go into designing and running a social media digital marketing campaign. You can always reach me for queries if at all any.

In case you have queries or as I have expressed earlier in this book, if you would like me to conduct a digital marketing or social media workshop or seminar, please feel free to reach me to know more. I will be more than glad to be of assistance.

If you enjoyed reading this book, would love to get your review and feedback too.

THANK YOU for your time.

Be Well

Ananth V
Life has a way of balancing itself!